The Mentor Within

Quiet reflections in a noisy world

www.PeterJohnsonOnline.com

The Mentor Within

Quiet reflections in a noisy world

Peter Johnson

Copyright

Project in Mind Limited, Berkeley Lodge, Moor Street,
Worcester, WR1 3DB, United Kingdom

Print Edition

British Library Cataloguing in Publication Data.

A catalogue record for this book is available from the British Library.

Parts originally published in 2011 as a private collection.

If we don't move, the horizon remains the same – often to enjoy, then comes a positive restlessness to encourage movement so we are always creating new horizons.

Cover: Crystallising from the SoulNotes Collection

The book cover is part of an original collection created by Louis Parson. He is the pioneer of a new form of art he calls SoulScapes, which celebrates and reach into the essence of who we are. You car view his work at www.LouisParsons.com

Contents

Introduction

This book has been created from many of the blogs that I have written and posted on my website:

PeterJohnsonOnline.com

and slightly edited here to form a text to challenge some of our everyday thinking.

In the whirlwind of daily life we can so quickly miss many of the things that can seem less important but, when we take some time to reflect, there are valuable messages to draw.

This book is not intended to be read at one sitting – more to be regularly dipped into and a chapter read that catches your eye or imagination. It does not have all the answers, and in many cases your own questions and answers will be more powerful than the ones written, I hope it becomes a catalyst for your own creativity. So make notes, write in the book and make it your own – there is plenty of white space to do so......it has been designed that way.

I have been asked about the message in 'creating new horizons', a term I have often used and the answer is quite simple. I was a competitive sports person and a keen favourite was the 400 metres and 400 metres hurdles – for those not too familiar with an athletics track, that is one lap.

As I have grown older, and I hope wiser, I came to realise that there is much to reflect on the 400 metres. The very first time I ran a 400 there was no training, no warm up, and no preparation. Just an instruction by the sports teacher, holding a stop, watch who bellowed: 'When I say **go** Johnson, run as fast as you can round the track and don't stop till you get back here.'

I did and it opened up a new world and a new metaphor:

"Life is a one lap race - with no practice lap and no lap of honour, even if we win!"

Perhaps that is why I love to discover or create new horizons.

Even on a flat running track your horizon changes until your focus is the winning tape. So there is always more to see, more to learn, more to experience – especially when your goal become clear.

So let's ensure every step on that lap a brilliant one. We won't get another chance.

Now unleash The Mentor Within…..

My best wishes,

Peter Johnson

Creating New Horizons

Tired, dusty and exhilarated - I've completed the challenge to trek to the top of Mount Vesuvius, Mount Stromboli, and Mount Etna over a five day period. It has been a privilege to trek with such a diverse and stimulating group of people, all motivated to assist a terrific cause, Meningitis Now.

We achieved our mission, and what a challenge it was! Vesuvius was the first and 'easy' one and got us into our stride with a fabulous ascent of this massively destructive volcano. It is amazing to see the damage and hideous destruction caused in Pompeii, which we looked at prior to our ascent. The volcanic ash was 20 metres deep in parts of Pompeii; it seemed inconceivable that such a huge amount of ash and volcanic material could have landed on the town from such a distance when looking at Vesuvius from the township. We trekked up the mountain through the forest and on to the volcano where we could see the differing coloured lava and ash still remaining. We were advised that this is a dormant volcano – long may it remain so.

Our next challenge was the trek up Stromboli. We got to the island following a hydrofoil journey from Sicily and it looked like the perfect volcano – straight out of the sea and a perfect cone shape, also with the characteristic cloud over the top. We started the climb pretty much as soon as we landed in the late afternoon. Even then the temperature of the day was still hot. We needed to drink large amounts of water to quench our thirst and to replenish the fluid level in our bodies, and clear the ever increasing dust levels. We reached the crater rim at about

8.30pm, when it was dark, to see a spectacular show of pyrotechnics. We had to put crash helmets on to ensure that any volcanic rock and lava that was thrown up did not hit us – not sure what use a hard hat was to red hot rock, but there had been no accidents so it was probably better not to ask! It was amazing to sit on the crater edge looking at the red lava bubbling away in the craters we could see. Periodically each crater would erupt into life and huge showers of red molten lava were blown into the sky. Very spectacular – also rather unnerving. We came down by sliding in the ash from the volcano. It was like sliding down a sand dune except there were about 3000 feet to go – the dust made visibility very poor and our head torches struggled through the low visibility. We got back down to sea level, and to the restaurant, in time for a very, very late dinner which was well earned. The first cold beer was wonderful.

Our next and final challenge took us to Mount Etna. This is a dramatically higher volcano with its peak at 3,300 metres which is a little over 11,000 feet. I hasten to add we did not climb the whole distance as we were transported by bus and then a very tough four wheel drive vehicle taking us well up the mountain. This was extremely well appreciated as the final ascent to the crater was an interesting challenge in itself. Visibility was poor, primarily because of the sulphur fumes billowing out from the crater which reduced our visibility and made it very difficult to breathe. Safety was clearly a factor throughout the challenge, no more so than on this final volcano. Once we had celebrated our success on 'peaking' the final volcano we then started our descent through volcanic debris, again a sliding and difficult descent of about 4500 feet. It was an amazing experience.

Mount Etna

3 volcanoes completed by 3 people who met in Tibet on another challenge. (Therein lies another story.) I am on the left, if you needed some help to work it out.

We all felt elated to have been involved with the challenge, which was certainly not easy. Each volcano was different from the others and we all had a significant feeling of self and team satisfaction at the end. All this for a great cause. We raised in excess of £75,000 and as I fully funded my trip **ALL** of what has kindly been gifted to me went straight to the charity to fund the fantastic work it does.

A thought for you….

I have been speaking at a business seminar recently about getting the most from yourself and your team for your business. This is critically important in these interesting times that we are experiencing. I am finding that relationships come under strain and also some self-limiting behaviours start to creep in, unnoticed. Are you finding this at a personal level or a business level? Many people are, and it is vital to consider what can be done.

Interestingly Carl Jung said:

> "Everything that irritates us about others can lead us to an understanding of ourselves."

So perhaps some questions to ask that will give you that focus...

1. How am I getting on with my colleagues at the moment?
2. Am I valuing what they do and letting them know?
3. Am I being valued for what I do?
4. Am I questioning my ability and if so, why?
5. Are we all very serious and the laughter levels have reduced?
6. What impact is my behaviour having on those people I care about away from work?

Just take a few minutes with that cup of coffee to ask yourself these questions. You are worth it aren't you?

Why not write your thoughts here............

Keeping our batteries well charged!

I have been very busy working on a project at the moment and slowly I realised I was being less effective. The time it took to do things was longer than usual. My mind was wandering. And still I pushed on. Then it struck me, I was not taking that time out to recharge my batteries. As tough as it was to leave the project unfinished I went to visit a friend.

We had a great lunch, shared a few stories since we last met and then took off into the mid afternoon air. It was great – the birds were chatting away, the autumn leaves were golden, the sky was fantastic with plump clouds sitting against a setting sun. We tramped down a lane, over a ford, up a hill, across a very muddy field, over an electric fence (which I discovered was very much 'on'…ouch!) past the church where the cows came to check us out, with their noses pushing though the fence. Then back for a steaming pot of tea – wonderful. Not a moment to think about that project, time invested in a great friendship. Wow what a treat……

And yes, the project did get finished and was much the easier and more fun after my 'time out'.

A question – what are you doing to keep your batteries well charged?

Training to keep an open mind

I was in London the other day visiting some clients and as the weather was good I decided I would walk as much as I could to enjoy the Christmas decorations and also get some exercise. I needed to cross the road at the junction of Oxford Street and Regent Street to get to the opposite diagonal point – nothing particularly unusual and I was expecting to cross Oxford Street first then cross Regent Street.

While I waited to cross I noticed that after the traffic halted at the red lights on Oxford Street the traffic started to move on Regent Street, so we pedestrians were kept waiting a little longer than I had anticipated. I was in no rush as my mind was clarifying some of the finer points of my upcoming meeting. Although, I noticed other pedestrians getting quite agitated as they thought the lights had missed out the signal. Then all of the traffic lights seemed to halt the traffic and the pedestrian lights turned to green so we could cross the road.

Now this is what interested me. I have used this junction many times and I started to cross Oxford Street with the intention of then having to cross Regent Street. But no – I could cross diagonally and complete the exercise in one go! Fascinating – also the road had been resurfaced with tarmac and a lighter surface that now made sense as it showed the diagonal route which I had barely noticed until then. This was a new development!

It certainly made me think and as I wended my way past John Lewis it got me mulling over all sorts of things and this is some of what I came up with:

1. Sometimes when we have to wait it can seem a waste of time, but in the end works out to take less time. How often are we rushing, feeling busy, when if we are more measured it can take less time?

2. Also do we use that waiting time usefully?

3. When we get used to something we can ignore new ways of looking at something. Are you ignoring new and better ways as you stick to the old?

4. If we are too blinkered we cannot see the new ways at all. How blinkered have you become in your business, in your life?

Fascinating questions which I am sure you can use to create that extra advantage. I am certainly training myself to keep an open mind and open eyes. Are you?

Are you keeping your head up?

For those of you who have been following my blog you will have noticed a trend which entails long walks. Something I love for many reasons, something I have been doing for many more years than I care to remember.

A key part of serious hill walking is having great footwear, and over the years I have worn out many boots. They become a trusted old friend and when it comes time to get a new pair, there are mixed feelings. The thought of pensioning off a reliable companion is always a concern.

Also, as technology has usually moved forward, there will be new products on the market, which is always interesting. In my time I have seen many ideas that have been simply daft, or styles better suited to the cat walk than a serious hill so I choose with care – my safety may be at risk if I don't, as I am not just a fair weather walker.

Whilst I love the old leather boots that a good treatment of wax will make waterproof I do admit that many of the new boots are just amazing. My latest version has 'memory foam' (whatever that is), a waterproof and breathable membrane, eyelets that hold the laces tight, a brilliant sole that is high grip and avoids the clogging of mud, and many more features that I won't bore you with.

My feet seem to be getting choosier as the years unfold, so it takes me a while to get comfortable in a new pair. The last few days I have been out 'breaking in' this new pair of mountain boots and, whilst they are mostly comfortable, the left one is making my foot ache – nothing odd and no blister, so I am feeling confident that they will be good.

Now what has his got to do with business? Well, I was walking at a fair old speed today, although my concentration was mostly on my left foot. I was well into my stride when a friendly voice hailed – 'hello Peter' – I had walked right past two people I know well. I stopped, apologised for my lack of recognition, and had a good conversation for about 15 minutes. We then set off on our way again.

It made me wonder - how often am I so absorbed with the things I am doing in my business, that I miss something else that could be an opportunity just sliding by? Now don't get me wrong, I think focus is vital if you are going to get the results you want. It just struck me though, that sometimes we are so self-consumed that we miss what may be a great opportunity.

After I left my friends I lifted my head up and concentrated on what was going on around me. Within a few minutes I had forgotten about my foot ache and really enjoyed seeing the day in a new light. The swans flying in formation overhead (now that is a powerful message for another day!), the changing sky that threatened snow again, the first signs of spring arriving and so much more. Now there was an interesting lesson that I had to relearn!

So what are you busy suffering, with your head down and attention elsewhere, which is possibly delivering you no results? What could you be capitalising on that is more valuable, if only you were paying attention?

Isn't a new month a good time to lift your eyes to your business horizon again?

I thought so!

Are you taking an optimistic view?

To get to one of my meetings today I had to walk some distance as there is no parking where I was going. The chill of winter is still with us and rather than rain, it was lightly sleeting when I set out. The sleet soon turned to rain. I was in good spirits and a little rain never causes much of a problem provided one is suitably wrapped up. As I walked along it was interesting looking at other people in the same circumstance. Some were appropriately dressed for this wet weather. Some were not. One thing that did strike me was the grim look on so many faces. Clearly the mood of their day was being influenced by the weather.

This got me thinking back to a time when I was on vacation, probably about 10 years ago. I had decided to have a major treat and go to Bermuda for a break. I had expected the weather to be wonderful, and it was for most of the time. My intention had been to do some diving but the sea had been churned up by a light storm the day before I landed so it certainly was not ideal conditions to see much underwater so I decided to give that venture a miss.

I do love walking and much to my surprise there was a lovely route from one end of the island to the other along the track of a disused railway. I set off in a pair of shorts and a tee shirt, only carrying my wallet and a small camera. Part way along my route it started to rain, which soon became a very heavy downpour and looked to be set in for quite some time. I was aware that my wallet and camera could easily become soaked with the rain, so popped into a nearby shop and asked if they could let me have a plastic bag – I thought it was clear from my sodden look that it was well and truly raining outside. The gentleman behind the counter asked "what is the matter?" I replied that it was raining heavily outside and didn't want to get my wallet and camera wet. At this point he went over to the window and looked out, and turning to me he said something that I shall never forget "Man, that's not rain, that's liquid sunshine!"

WOW!! what optimism, and I must say since that day I have never viewed rain in the same way. It has been a wonderful lesson that has carried me through many trying events and one I do reflect on and ask myself how I could view the positive when so many could view the negative.

So my question to you:

'What are you screwing your face against when with a little optimistic thinking you could create a fantastic new perspective?'

Oh, and by the way I did get my plastic bag after a brilliant conversation.

Snowdrops – new beginnings

I was in a friend's garden, on the border of England and Wales, a little over a week ago and I was amazed at the sheer carpet of snowdrops that welcomed me at every turn. These wonderful little plants are a delightful sight and start the new season of flowers and growth. It is so late for these to still be in flower – although with a winter that has been colder and lasted longer than we have grown accustomed, it is hardly surprising. A pleasant surprise I would add. The news today reported that magnolia trees are a month behind.

I am sure that nature will tidy up our growing diary and if it doesn't, there is little that we can do to encourage things.

The snowdrops always make me think of the awakening of nature and her getting into full stride.

We may have set our goals for the New Year and then along comes these delightful little flowers to remind us of new growth. Perhaps new growth that we should be creating in our own lives! In our own businesses! In our own community!

It certainly got me thinking about what I could, should, and would do. I hope it has given you a nudge too!

My good wishes for your growth.

'Work life blend'

Last weekend I was out walking near the River Severn in Gloucestershire, England, with a friend I had not seen for a while. We had lots of great conversation to catch up on. It was a rather impromptu walk as we had both been busy in our worlds of work and neither of us had been out walking in the mud for a while. Also, as we live in different parts of the country we can always make the excuse that it is not easy. A grabbed opportunity saw us munching some lovely French pastries and drinking hot spiced juice by our cars prior to setting off.

The term 'work life balance' has been gaining ground for some years. It is meant to recognize the need to balance our work with other parts of our life. This walk got me thinking about the phrase I use, rather than this misused term.

I have to confess that the term 'work life balance' has never sat comfortably with me even though it is in wide use.

Why, you may ask? Well, it is rather simple really. If you think of a set of old fashioned scales with the weights placed on one side with the item to be weighed on the other you can conjure up a good picture. So, with this in mind if you put more work into one scale pan, you have to put more non-work activities into the other pan. Likewise, if you put less work into one pan the other pan needs less non-work activity to make it balance. This is just daft.........I hope you agree!

Also, it makes work and non-work two very different things – they are both a part of who we are. Over the past few years I have coined the phrase *'work life blend'*. This to me is what it is about. The blend of life with work. Work is a part of who we are and we should be proud of what we do, whatever that is. I have seen people who are so proud and brilliant at what they do. I have seen others scrape through and have no pride. That applies no matter whether they are fulfilling a less skilled role or from a skilled professional or craft background.

We should never feel guilty about our work and feel the need to 'balance the scales'. Yes, we ought to be respectful of our use of time with those who are part of our lives, although to my mind that is a very different thing. Some people in parts of the world have a massively tough time and work is vital to sustain life at the basic level. That is why for those who are more fortunate, creating that blend should be what we strive for.

The walk by the River Severn last weekend was a great part of my blend……..so are you creating a balance, or a blend in your life?

The 'big top'

I always enjoy writing my articles as it usually means something has caught my attention. Well, life has been very busy of late with client work, enjoying the wonderful spring weather and a series of meetings. Rather an interesting follow-on from my blog on 'work life blend'.

The other day I was out walking and noticed that a circus had arrived in town and the colourful 'big top' had already been erected.

It got me thinking about the fun and pleasure that circuses provide to the many people who go to see what amazing antics the performers get up to.

It also got me thinking about the serious business that they must be to remain viable. Almost a contradiction in the fun versus the serious.

With this circus it struck me how smart everything was too, the big top, the box office, the vehicles were all clean and bright, everything look great, right down to the signs that they used. Also, after they had left there was no mess, no litter, no sign that they had been there.

Clearly these people took their business very seriously and made sure that they gave a great impression, looked the part and left with their reputation intact.

Now for a serious business question – do you?

Mistakes that create opportunity

On Saturday I met up with some friends at Oxford, England, and spent a great day chatting away and enjoying a long walk. It was raining when we first met at the railway station so a coffee stop was a good first point of call, hoping the rain would stop. It didn't, but keen to get on with our day we wrapped up well and set off.

During the early part of our walk I relayed the story that I have shared in an earlier post under the title 'Are you taking an optimistic view?'

We soon came to a church that was a planned interest point and enjoyed looking around and speaking to the two ladies that were busy keeping the place in top condition. A delightful church it was too and an interesting stained glass window as you can see from the picture. If you are interested in cars, it is a Morris Minor, which was built at the nearby Cowley factory of Morris, during the 1950s and 1960s, a name now lost in the mists of British motoring heritage. It also transpires that their new organ is by the same maker of the more recent organ in Worcester Cathedral – interesting as I live near the cathedral. So, a fascinating stop on our walk – made all the more interesting perhaps by discovering we were in the wrong church…..

We were directed to the church we were looking to start our walk from by one of the ladies and set off on our way. The church we were looking for is where C S Lewis, the author, is buried, one of only a few people to gain a triple first from Oxford University. Also where another fascinating stained glass window is housed, but that is a different story.

It is so easy to get annoyed with the wasted time and false start to miss the opportunity that this mistake has caused. Interestingly, none of us were at all agitated by the error. In fact we were pleased that we had seen the first church, shared some words with kindly people and learnt more in the process.

So how often have you started somewhere only to realize it was at the wrong place……or was it?

What have you ringing in your ears......?

The sky was blue, the air fresh and the sun brightening everything up on a wonderful quintessentially English morning. I was walking along the river bank near Worcester Cathedral and it was a delight to see families out early with the children playing quietly or feeding the swans on the river. Also the air was filled with the ringing of the bells from the Cathedral.

Apparently the bells are one of the best 'rings' in the world. A sound so familiar. A sound so stirring. A sound that I have heard so many times. Sadly, so often the pace of life means we do not stop the mental 'noise' that blocks out the splendid skill of the bell ringers, and the majesty of the bells themselves. The ringers stopped and then started again with a new peal – it was wonderful to enjoy the sound, in such a perfect setting, on such a glorious day. They did this three times and each different peal certainly lifted my spirits.

It got me thinking about the bells of Birmingham Cathedral, which I had heard only a few weeks before. This time it was in the early evening and I was taking the time to stroll through the city and enjoy the very pleasant feeling of being well ahead of time for once, so able to enjoy the moment. I was on my way to an award ceremony and speeches for Chartered Managers – I feel privileged to be one of the thousand or so who are so qualified across the world and I knew an interesting evening lay in store. After a hectic day, it was good to feel relaxed and open to the evening ahead, rather than stressed and tired like so many people end their working day.

It got me thinking that in the fast pace of daily life.....

- How often do we fail to hear what is going on around us?

- How often do we fail to hear what people say?

- How often do we make decisions based on what we think someone has said, when in reality we have failed to have really listened at all?

The double edge to these questions is that we can be equally deaf at work and at home.

So how would you answer the questions?

I know how I should answer them. And with that thought humbly ringing in my ears I will aim to try to listen more often. Will you?

Are you always present with your clients?

It has been a wonderful day with brilliant sunshine and generally people feeling very uplifted. One of the beauties of the British Isles is that we have some wonderful weather, albeit to listen to the average conversation anyone would think otherwise. I love the changing seasons, the relative unpredictability of it all and the fact that as the year unfolds so does the changing scenery, type of clothes we wear, the food we eat, the drinks we drink.

Yes, there are some events that cause pain and problems but compared with other parts of the world we are very fortunate. Now this is not a ramble about the weather – a subject always on the tongues of many a 'Brit'. No, this is more about our attitude and the impact it has. But please bear with me so you get the theme of the issue.

I have been working long days all week and whilst I had some work to do today, it was more about getting a few jobs done and errands run. I set off fairly early this morning as I had a fair list to complete, so by about 10.30am I was ready for a well earnt pause. So I decided to stop at a favourite cafe where they have tables and chairs on the pavement <u>and</u> in the shade.

Whilst I do like the sun, I can get a good 'British Tan' (pink) if I am not careful. I also had a copy of the daily paper, which I wanted to have a look through. Now one of the things I like about this cafe is that the service is always good, although never speedy, unless specifically asked for. The benefits are three fold – firstly I get to read more of my paper, secondly I can people watch for a little longer, and thirdly everything is prepared fresh.

My usual preference is for a large black coffee and a croissant. In most brand named establishments the coffee is equally as good but the croissant is cold and served plain.

In this cafe a large cup of steaming coffee arrives shortly after a plate has been placed with a thick white napkin and knife. Some while later a basket arrives lined with another thick white napkin together with its' contents of a freshly baked croissant, some butter and a small jar of preserve with the red and white check top – just wonderful. The people serving are always delightful, and interestingly the price is no different from the other places, so you can see why I prefer this cafe.

The interesting part of today came from the gentleman who served me. He was charming and looked after me very well, he came and took the order, prepared that table with the plate, brought my coffee, brought the croissant and received payment (and a tip). But, and it is an interesting but, in the conversation that was part of our interchange he was clearly wishing he was not at work due to the weather. "I'd be even better if I wasn't' here on a day like today."

My next point of call elicited a very similar comment from the delightful young lady who looked after me as I quivered and quavered about an article I was looking at.

As I continued with my errands it made me ponder a few thoughts:

- The service I had received was first class.

- Just a few words had made me feel a little uneasy.

Had I allowed those words to make me feel uneasy and take the edge off each event? And if so, why?

The answer to these questions was very clear – I was no longer the focus of their attention – their wish to be elsewhere was.

And perhaps most importantly it turned the mirror back on me:

What do I say that may make others feel uneasy, and make me appear to be less present with my clients?

Now that is a question I **will** give some thought to. Will you?

Lion ahead! I nearly missed you….

I was in Trafalgar Square in London last week and it was busy as usual. People from many parts of the world were taking pictures of each other in front of the famous fountains and lions. I was walking at some speed, as usual, from the tube station to a favourite café of mine that overlooks the square. It was a wonderful summer's day and I decided to stop for a few minutes and take in some of the relaxed atmosphere of the early morning.

I was in a business suit, wearing one of my colourful ties and carrying a briefcase. When I stopped I got out a camera and took a few pictures, one of which you can see here. Because I had stopped and was taking pictures I was approached by a number of people to take pictures of them in front of the fountain and lions, with their cameras. I had ceased to be the busy 'city gent' and was now approachable to help them capture the memories to be shared when they returned to their homes.

Eventually I headed over to the café to enjoy my coffee after a very early start and it got me thinking. I came up with three main thoughts:

1. Some things are consistent, day in day out, week in week out, year in year out and we take them for granted. If we stop and look we sometimes enjoy what we had lost sight of. (In my case it was the lions – they have been there since I can remember and they are amazing statues, frequently sat upon by visitors to have their picture taken. In my familiarity I was not seeing.)

2. When you stop people see you and speak – and a smile can cross any language barrier.

3. A small gesture such as taking someone's picture can make someone's day.

So, what amazing things are you so familiar with that you no longer see? When was the last time you stopped, smiled and perhaps spoke to someone new?

And thirdly, is there anything that you can do to make someone's day?

You know the answers, just as I did when I stopped – now take action.

Taking time out….

I have rather neglected my blog post for the past couple of months, and feel a little guilty. Partly because I have been prompted to 'get back on the case' by some people who follow my articles. And partly because I get great pleasure as they make me think about my life, my business and importantly my clients

I have had a very interesting summer as I decided to spend time in South America. Mostly being based on the shores of Lake Titicaca in Bolivia – a rather remote part of the world. But as you can see from the picture it is stunningly beautiful. It has provided me with some interesting material to reflect upon which I will be sharing with you over the coming months.

.s also been an excellent opportunity to recharge my batteries. Jo hope that you have taken the opportunity to recharge your batteries and, importantly, enjoy some time with the people you care about.

So let us resume the questions we should be asking ourselves to make us the best we can be. The best we can be for ourselves, for those we are close to and for those we serve as we roam through this journey of life to create new horizons.

Why questions? Because if you are asked a question you answer it, don't you?

And who better to ask the questions you need to answer than............well you decide!

Is your pressure correct…?

In my last post I mentioned that I had been spending time over the summer in South America. One of the interesting points I noticed on my travels was to do with the change that occurs with altitude. Anyone who has flown will have seen what happens to an empty plastic bottle between cruising at altitude and landing, even though the aircraft is pressurised. It rather surprised me when this happened to such an extreme extent when on land.

I had been staying by Lake Titicaca, which is about 4,000 metres high (that's about 13,000ft), and it takes a while to get used to the thin air. To put that into perspective, the highest mountain in England is 978 metres and in the British Isles 1344 metres. If you have not been at altitude it is humbling to realize that you can no longer walk at the same speed and you get out of breath very quickly until you have acclimatised, so things have to be done more slowly.

Once I had acclimatised, traveling over one of the high passes I met the llama in the picture. This was at 5,700 metres (18,500ft). I took a drink of water from a plastic bottle, which I emptied. I put it back in my rucksack and thought little more about it. When I took it out to throw away it was almost flat from the increased pressure lower in the mountains. Interesting, I thought. So what happens to our bodies as we change altitude?

Now this got me thinking about a range of things. How we perform under pressure. How too much pressure can flatten us and ruin our performance. But, and this was a big BUT for me, how too little pressure does not allow us to perform at our best. The thin air slows one's body down, the thin air slows one's mind down, and the thin air means that we are well, slower. So:

- Do you have enough pressure to keep you moving?

- Do you have enough pressure to keep your sharp? Or…

- Do you have too much pressure which is flattening your performance?

Now those are questions to really make you think….unless you are at too high an altitude.

Are you forgetting the effort you put in….?

What a lovely autumn day here in England. Just perfect with a clear blue sky, the onset of the autumn colours from the trees, the crispness in the air to keep refreshed and invigorated once one has got into a decent pace for walking.

Early this morning I heard, and then saw, a hot air balloon high in the sky over my back garden and what a lovely spectacle it made. I am sure it was a delight for those on board too. So I was rather surprised to see another one, in fact two, this afternoon taking to the skies when I was on one of my walks between the tasks I was working on. It is so easy to forget to make the effort and take a well earned break, and mine was well rewarded.

The balloons made me think about what I do, and sometimes fail to keep doing. There is a lot of preparation that goes into launching a hot air balloon, much more than a casual thought really gives. Forgetting all of the preparation before arriving at site - such as purchase, training to be a pilot, weather forecasts and arranging for the due time and place of departure – there is a lot of activity on the ground. Activity also by people who don't even get to take the flight, who then have to make sure they are at the point of landing too!

The sheer effort of getting the balloon ready for inflating and then launch is considerable. Once in the air, in flight, the wind will determine which direction you are going. There is only the periodic use of the burner to heat more air to keep the balloon at the desired altitude. Also the amount of fuel used to maintain altitude seems to be much less than the roaring flames to get the balloon airborne in the first place.

Now the simple questions that these sights in the sky asked of me were:

1. What have I put all the effort into and just not put that final puff of hot air to make the difference? The difference to get airborne?

2. Where am I failing to keep the burners aflame to keep the altitude correct?

3. Where perhaps should I accept I am out of fuel and arrange a suitable landing – either temporary, or permanently?

4. What should I start to do to create new skills, new opportunities, new views of new horizons?

Now those are tough questions and over the next couple of miles of walking it really did make me consider my preparation, my attitude and, importantly, my altitude.

Are you flying high?

Perhaps now is a good time to puff some hot air into that question!

Team work and trust...

What a lovely autumn we are having with such a fantastic range of colours starting to appear on the trees before they shed their leaves for the winter. It seems to have brought so many people out and I was pleased to see much activity on the River Severn too (the longest river in the United Kingdom at 354 km). It was quite early and already there were various boats on the river.

As I walked along there was a dragon boat moving well on the river to the beat of a drum. All of the people on board were dressed in similar red tops, so it was clearly a team. They seemed to be in training as no other boat of a similar type was about – they were all trying hard as the boat would speed, then slow whilst a briefing was made before starting off again at pace. The drum beater beating out a rhythm.

There were a few canoeists about and a number of rowing boats as well. The one in the picture caught my attention, as it was also a team in training rather than competition – this is a 'coxed eight'. So, eight rowers plus a 'cox'.

Unlike the canoeists or the dragon boat racers, everyone in an 'eight' faces the opposite direction from which they are going. Well, with the exception of one person in this boat, who is called the cox. The cox does not row, their role is to steer and get the best route, to call out the rowing speed and deploy the best tactics to win over rivals.

This always strikes me as being a brilliant opportunity to get it all wrong. OR, to work as a fantastic team and get it right.

Typically, the cox is the one person who is least able to row. The main attribute of a rower is strength and stamina. The cox also tends to be smaller, to avoid handicapping the team with excess weight. Now this is not a lesson on the layout of a crew in a boat, although anyone who has seen a rowing 'eight' will know that they tend to be pretty strong people (female or male). This is more about realizing that everyone has to be excellent at what they do:

- The strength and stamina of the rowers

- The skill to keep your stoke in time, else oars could collide with devastating effect

- The technical aspect of each rowing stroke

- The correct tempo being signalled by the cox

- The direction of the boat to miss competitors, to miss troublesome parts of the river, to miss the river bank

This list could go on with so much more but I think you have the idea.

Now how does all this work? I think it is quite profound:

- It is the ability to be excellent at what you do, at an individual level

- It is the commitment to the team, to be your best for the team

- Crucially, it is the trust to do what you are excellent at, whilst trusting others to do what they are excellent at.

If any part of this is wrong, the whole does not work – if you are one of the oars and are not fit or accurate, the whole of the boat will feel unbalanced, if you are the cox and choose the wrong tempo or the wrong route to steer, you all fail to get the result.

1. Now for any team you are part of, or run:

2. Are you all excellent at what you do?

3. Do you keep fit for the tasks in hand?

4. And, most critically, have you developed the trust in your team to ensure that you all get on and do what you are there to do?

5. If not, what training are you doing to correct things?

6. What honest debriefings do you have to build that trust for yourself and for the team?

Now these are powerful questions and if the answers are all affirmative, perhaps your team performance will be as powerful as a top performing 'coxed eight'. Even if, as one of the oars, you cannot see where you are going because you trust the person steering implicitly.

Now that is a top performing team....!

I'll leave you to steer your team to the winning line.

The first Business School in the UK.....

Last week I returned to Henley Business School, where I am an alumnus and studied for my first Masters Degree. It was wonderful to turn off the road and follow the drive over the meadow where cows were grazing in the morning sun, on a lovely crisp day. One of the cows chose, at that moment, to amble slowly across the drive so I had to stop. This gave me an opportunity to stop and look rather than rush.

Henley Business School is set on the edge of the River Thames, just a short distance from the town where the world famous rowing regatta takes place every year. It was the first Business School in the United Kingdom and has always been one of the top performing schools across the world – this is a special place indeed.

Since I graduated I have frequently returned, always aiming to attend at least once per year, albeit it was a little longer than usual this time. As always there is progress and this time was certainly no exception. After a delightful and valuable meeting, I spent a little time walking around the grounds, something that was common practice when studying there. Something that was, and still is, an integral part of Henley learning. The conversations with like minded business students from all over the world created a rich experience, an experience that I value to this day. Also there was time for reflection in such a beautiful setting.

Now this last point got me thinking about the speed with which our worlds spin. And that is when I realized something. Away from the usual fast pace of life and taking some time to reflect again made me remember why places such as Henley are so effective – they make us focus on the matter in hand.

If we are investing time away from the hum of daily life, time away from people we care about, we really do make sure that time counts – we do make sure there is focus on what we are there to do. The fact there are fewer distractions is all part of the rich experience.

Now this is something that I will admit to periodically forgetting, falling into the 'more haste less speed' trap, so, I shall be taking more time to focus.

This one single action, **focus**, is what differentiates the highly successful from the less successful people. Apparently, the average person has between 2,500 – 3,000 thoughts per day whilst the most successful have fewer than 1,200. Because they focus and don't get distracted – interesting…..

Now are you going to get caught up in the 'noise' of daily life, or are you going to focus too?

Food for thought, and a thought that needs action!

Are you on the correct road…..?

I was recently in the countryside walking with a friend and, as you can see from the picture, it was just before the autumn colours set in. It was a magnificent day and the walk was equally as good too. We came across this wonderful old road with the trees arching over, and it was as straight as any Roman road. Interestingly, although it was clearly a very old road, it was in good shape and had some very light use. I guess, most from walkers and farm machinery. It was totally clear which way we were going, with no opportunity to stray from this part of the walk. On one side was a very old hedge with an old wall on the other to keep us on the 'straight and narrow' or perhaps put a better way, on the 'chosen route'.

When walking in good company it is all too easy to stray from the path that was intended, only to have to retrace steps or find an alternative path. This happens in business too, if there is a route map in place and you stray it is easy to realize and then get back on track. So often in business though, I find that no business plan has been written at all – let alone used as a route map. Would you start out on a walk with no idea of where you are going – probably not, is my guess. So why try and run a business with no route map – no business plan?

In this short article all I wanted to do was ask the question – are you on the correct road?

If you are unsure, do have a look at the publication Business Plan on a Page (details at the end of the book), it may just help you keep on your 'chosen route'.

In the cold light of day…..

Over the past few weeks we have been experiencing some very cold weather and snow in the UK. This has caused problems for many people as they try and go about their daily routines. For some it has stopped many of their activities.

I visited a friend yesterday who has only just started to surface after 3 weeks of deep snow and impassable roads to her home. Whilst there are many 'down sides' to this weather there are also some positives too, if we care to take stock. These are just a few ideas….

- The opportunity of cancelled meetings or activities that provide a wonderful 'gift of time' to complete other things that have been waiting to be done – often for too long.

- The camaraderie that many have displayed during this time of a shared problem.

- The change in scenery so we see things in a different light.

- The resourcefulness of having to make do with what we have rather than always being able to go out and get everything that we think is crucial for our existence.

…..I am sure you can think of more, can't you?

I was out walking the other day and took the picture you see. It is part of the River Severn that flows through Worcester, in England, and it is frozen over. In many parts of the world a frozen river is nothing exceptional – in England it is. It froze over on Christmas Eve when the temperature in Worcester dropped to minus 19C, and remained well below freezing for a few days. It is a wonderful sight and got me thinking about how we see our world.

We often see all the colours and different shading, the picture being complex. This picture is completely devoid of colours other than on a scale from white, through grey to black. Interesting and very impactful, I am sure you agree. By the way, it is a colour picture not black and white.

It got me thinking that how often do we strip away the complex and bring our situation into focus by looking at it through a simpler lens? Sometimes you see things you had not seen before, sometimes you can see the framework of the situation and realise where the weak points are.

Interesting…..and especially useful as I create my goals.

Now I am going to look at the framework and overall structure of those goals to make sure they are robust and will ensure I am going to be successful.

To make sure that I don't just create dreams and no reality.

As you set your goals are you going to keep that focus too? I do hope so.

What footprints are you leaving…..?

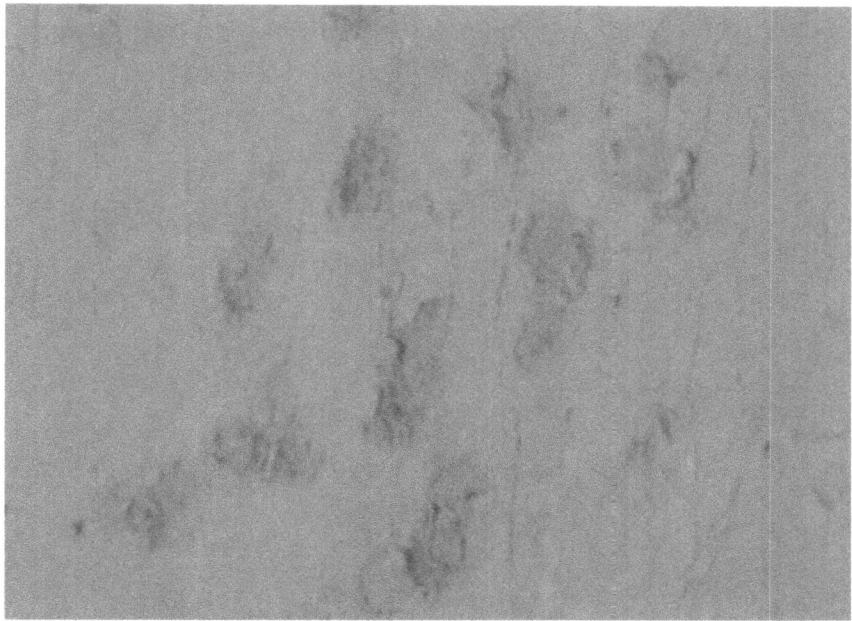

The attached picture may not seem very interesting at first sight although that should not put you off. If you look again you will see some indentations in the surface. They are in fact dinosaur footprints from about 60 million years ago. The impressions are in the surface of rock right in the middle of a cement factory. When the rock was being excavated they were found and fortunately preserved – this was in the mid 1990s.

The finding is one of the largest discoveries and collection of dinosaur footprints anywhere in the world, and a large variety of different types too. Over 5,000 footprints have been found at this site. Prior to that less than 100 footprints had been found at one site anywhere else in the world. So what a fantastic discovery – that could so easily have been turned into cement!

It is interesting to learn that over a huge period of time the mud where the dinosaurs trod became covered with silt and sediment. Eventually, with the change in the shape of the earth's crust they were forced up at an angle of 70 degrees from the flat surface, where all those millions of years ago these great creatures roamed.

It is incredible to think how these footprints survived the giant forces in the earth that drove up this land from near sea level, and on a flat surface, to form part of the Andes range of mountains in South America. The footprints are now at 2750 metres (9,000feet) and it has been proven that they would have been near sea level – just incredible! Sadly, it is likely now that they have been found, they will disintegrate over a fairly short time.

I have been fortunate to see this amazing sight. I allowed my mind to wonder and wander at just what it would have been like when these creatures roamed the earth. It is also fascinating to think that these creatures have enthralled people of all ages over the years. Interestingly, not so very long ago I met someone (an adult) who lived in a part of the world where they had never heard of dinosaurs. When these creatures were explained and pictures from books shown to the person, visualising what they probably looked like, the imagination and surprise was amazing.

So here we have two interesting thoughts to dwell on and, I hope, take action:

1. From the last point, what do we not know that would be amazing to find out? This may sound like an odd thing to say, but if we continue learning and developing, taking interest in things around us and being inquisitive, who

knows what we may find out that we never knew anything about before. All adding to our personal and professional development. A journey of lifelong learning that an open mind will embrace – so how open is your mind?

2. And the second thought. Do you want to leave anything behind you that could be interesting to others who follow? If yes, what could that be and are you taking action already?

We all leave footprints, how long will yours last….?

What obstacles are in your way?

I was early for a meeting so it was lovely to take my time and see what was around the place I was visiting. It is always far more rewarding than rushing in with seconds to spare and then rushing out to our next commitment.

It was a cold and very sunny morning and I came across this obstacle area for children shown in the picture. It was very well kept, all of the equipment seemed in top condition. As it was early in the morning, icy and a school day I was not surprised to see little activity.

The thing that struck me straight away was how similar it was to many such courses that are used for management development and leadership development. Many has been the time that I have either undertaken exercises or put others through their management development paces.

It also made me smile that so often we forget what was learnt at such times, only to have to scamper over the obstacles again.

We so often forget what has been learnt and decide to get from A to B by making ourselves climb over the same obstacles in our work, in our life, in our career.........that really should be avoided.

On this day it would have required careful footwork to avoid slipping on the icy steps. Our hands would need to be well gloved to avoid the biting cold as we held onto each piece of equipment. Our attention would be focussed on the detail of where next to put our feet and hands. Our concentration would be needed to avoid being distracted and falling over.

Now:

- How often have we needed to tread carefully for fear of upsetting things?

- Had our hands so well gloved and lost the 'feel' of what was needed?

- Focussed on the detail when the big picture and far vision was required of us?

- Concentrated so hard that we failed to notice the important distraction, and fallen over anyway?

And perhaps the biggest question – how often have we chosen to look at everything in our line of sight, only see the obstacles, then start to tackle them like some sort of new assault course...........when we could have and should have looked wider and taken the easy path around the obstacles?

So....

- Are you only seeing obstacles and don't have confidence in what you already know?

- Who are you asking to help you, or are you that 'lone ranger' tackling the obstacles when someone could help you see the easier and faster path?

Now these ARE two interesting questions to help you.....or you could choose the obstacle course after all!

Are you creating the right first impression?

I was out with a friend yesterday and doing a little browsing around some shops when I came across something that caught my eye. The person running the shop was delightful, very helpful letting us have a good look around, not pestering, helpful in supporting our growing interest.

The item that caught my eye was not too expensive, but certainly more than a casual whim purchase. It was also more of a 'want' than a 'need' purchase. Therefore, I was inclined to consider my possible expenditure before getting to a stage when I was about to part with some money. It was a cold, dull day and mid morning, so it seemed that an interlude to enjoy a hot cup of coffee and consider the possible purchase would be a good idea. I was in no rush and out to enjoy the day. Sometimes to prolong the decision on a purchase makes the satisfaction all the more – I am sure you agree.

Over coffee I discussed the merits of the item and ended up very enthusiastic to make the purchase. So, after coffee, we headed back over the road to the shop, not noticing the rain, with a spring in my step. The helpful and pleasant young man was no longer there. The person we met on entering barked a polite but curt 'welcome'. Instantly I did not feel valued or wanted, nor did the friend I was with – so it was not just my response. Even though the person was well spoken, well presented and probably the owner of the shop - the mood had changed.

Within 30 seconds we were back out on the street. We could not get out of the shop fast enough. The anticipation of looking at the item and holding it again, this time with every intent on purchase.......was gone. We were empty handed and heading back to the car to continue on our journey.

A lost opportunity for the shop owner. A strange feeling that the item no longer held the magic it had only a short while ago – all because of the greeting, lack of warmth and lack of a true genuine welcome.

Now this got me thinking about the first impression WE make when we meet someone. In our private lives, in our business lives.

So, what impression are you making?

A serious question I am sure you agree!

Now if you were that shop owner, did you realise what had happened? Would you be properly welcoming next time someone came through the door? Or just bemoaning the lack of business when people like me go elsewhere?

We all know the saying that 'you don't get a second opportunity to make a first impression'. I have a rather deeper 'take' on this which is included in a publication you may find very useful called 'First Impressions – A Special Report For You And Your Business', which also includes two valuable checklists (further details are at the end of this book).

If the man who lost the sale yesterday had invested in my special report he would be well in profit by now!

Look again…..

I took the picture you can see here standing in a similar position, on the bank of the River Severn, in England, that I posted on 31 December in the article called "In the cold light of day..." also in this book.

The earlier picture appears to be black and white, even though it was taken in full colour. This was due to the severe cold in the winter and the river being completely frozen over (something I had never seen before).

This later picture shows how the English spring is starting so well with wonderful hues of green bursting from the buds on the trees. The light has a freshness too, with the sun casting a vibrancy of colour not seen in the earlier picture.

It is amazing how different things look even from the same position – it is the conditions that have changed, the season has changed, and perhaps I can see things now that I either didn't, or could not see before.

I find this happens so often when I take a new look at an old opportunity or an old problem. New eyes can create new images. New thoughts and new perspectives can abound. It also reminds me of the quotation from Heraclities, which goes something along the lines of:

"When a person enters a river for the second time it is neither the same river nor are they the same person."

This reflection through words always makes me stop and think.

How has the issue changed? How have I changed?

At the moment this is highly pertinent as I am developing a major new programme and revisiting much of my material ....which I am now appreciating with new eyes, new understanding and a new richness.

Perhaps there is something that you need to reflect on again:

- A business issue

- A personal issue

- A relationship issue

- …..or just taking time to look with a new perspective at things that you may have taken for granted.

Perhaps your river has changed. Perhaps you have changed too.

Food for thought....

I was having coffee with my sister-in-law the other day, at a delightful café which we occasionally use. We sat outside as we wanted to watch the world go by while we chatted, even though it was quite cool. It was mid morning and I had eaten an early breakfast so I ordered a bacon sandwich with my coffee.

I've had bacon sandwiches at a wide variety of places ranging from simple cafés, to decent hotels. Many good, some indifferent and the occasional one very poor. Today's was exceptional, certainly one of the best I have ever had. So much so that after checking that it wasn't only the appearance that was good – a large bite confirmed it tasted good too – I took the attached picture. The picture shows the splendid offering in all its glory, including evidence of my quality testing!

Now this got me thinking at how often we are surprised by the quality of the service or product we are purchasing. My guess is most of the time it is about what we expect, and it therefore becomes a mere commodity. Sometimes it is below the standard we were expecting, and we may grumble a little, probably just to ourselves, and then progress on our way.

Sometimes it is well below what we were expecting and we will either complain, or decide not to buy from this supplier again.

It is rare we have our expectations exceeded – when we do it is such a delight, as it was on this lovely spring morning. A comment of praise was soon passed to the person looking after us.

Now this got me thinking about the services or products we are buying on a regular basis. Are we happy or have we got into a rut of accepting mediocrity? Not really happy but not disappointed enough to either discuss the issue with the provider, or change.

It also got me thinking about the service I provide to my clients – am I still delighting them? Perhaps I need to ask them, rather than assume that they will let me know if I am letting my standard drop or if I am not upping my game for them to remain delighted.

So are you asking some questions:

- Am I getting services and products I am really happy with?

- If I am not happy, have I discussed it with the people who could change things?

- If the service is exceptional have I thanked them?

- Are my services and products seen as a commodity, or are they delighting the people I serve?

- Do I need to ask my customers or clients if they are happy?

- What else could I do to make the impact of what I do exceptional?

And perhaps some more questions of your own will come to mind too as you ponder on the ones above.

Food for thought – well it was once I had finished such a wonderful sandwich. I hope it feeds your mind enough to seek some answers too.

Yes, white can mean black....

I was in London recently and it is a city where the quality of the taxi drivers is renown – in a very positive way I add! They have to complete something called 'The Knowledge', this is learning the whereabouts of a significant number of places, many historic – plus the location of some 25,000 streets in a 6 mile radius of Charring Cross Station, in central London. This is required so they use the best route to take their passengers – called 'fares'. A test that has been in place since 1865 and is the world's most demanding course for taxi drivers.

The taxis are known as 'black cabs' in much the same way that taxis in New York are yellow. I was waiting at a set of traffic lights ready to cross the road when the taxi cab pictured drew up

– I was rather slow in getting my camera out of my briefcase and taking the picture, so by the time I was ready the lights had changed – hence part is missing. It may not be the best picture but it made me think about our use of common terms. London taxis are known as 'black cabs' irrespective of colour. And I think this one is as far from black as we can get! The majority are still black but there are other colours too, silver, burgundy, yellow to mention some others.

Now this got me thinking further about terms that are used that probably, to a stranger, make no sense. A black cab – but it is white!

On my way across London for a friendly meeting, I caught the underground train, called 'the tube'. We were just leaving one of the stations that are above ground, when I overheard a fellow passenger who was visiting from Australia. He was speaking, by mobile phone, to someone he was arranging to meet soon. 'I am on the train' he said – it was clear from the following comments that he had caused the other person some anxiety.

'No, I am on the train' he repeated. Now, to a Londoner this means that you are not on the 'tube', more likely on a train heading out of London. It was clear they were meeting outside a 'tube station' some stops down the line. Fortunately, before the phone signal was lost, he was able to reassure his friend that he was on the right method of transport and not heading off into some other part of Britain, 'on the train'. Albeit he was rather puzzled as he mentioned to me – 'He asked if I was on the underground but I could see daylight. He says I am not on a train but it looks like a train from where I come from.' He had a good point!

So, how often do we use a term that to someone <u>not</u> in 'the know', or without 'the knowledge', may fail to understand?

More crucially though, how often do we use a term that means something different to someone else. At times this may be even worse because they may not seek clarification and we may not realise our message has been misunderstood. I fear I may do it more often than I realise – is there a possibility that you could make the occasional assumption too?

Food for thought as I head off for lunch – which some people call dinner – whilst others call dinner, supper!

Oh! And by the way I think a 'tube' to an Australian is a can of larger, or is it beer?

Are you using your senses....?

As you are aware, I love walking and was out yesterday evening on The Malvern Hills which I find to be a very special place. It is here that Sir Edward Elgar is said to have gained inspiration for many of the enigmatic pieces of music he composed. As I was getting into my stride I came across these glorious bluebells. They are such a wonderful flower that sadly only last for a short time. Mostly, they grow under the shade of trees as you can see here.

It reminded me that in the UK we are well into the spring season – with all of the wonderful new colours and long days that are part and parcel of this time of year. The colour of these flowers is so rich, and with so many flowers packed into such an area it is always a special sight.

The picture conveys some of what I saw, the smell is impossible to replicate – in the early evening it is a heavy perfume that hangs under the trees, just so fragrant. I stopped to take the picture, and I also wanted to stand and breathe in this special sent of nature too. By stopping and standing I also heard the birds chattering away, already making their nests ready for the new chicks that will all too soon bring the start of summer.

As I stood there it made me question how often I stop and consider what is happening around me – and importantly using all of my senses. People ask us 'does that make sense?' – how often do we use **all** of our senses when we answer? We usually fire back an answer ready to move on.

So:

- Would it be valuable to stop once in a while and use more of our senses when we are considering that decision?

- Perhaps – are we too busy rushing not wanting to stop…..and then miss something that could have been important? Some things, like the bluebells, don't stay around for long.

- Are we finding the time to enjoy them?

Well, perhaps Elgar was onto something – perhaps that is why these wonderful hills keep calling me back – perhaps that is why I have found the time to write this article!

By a nose……

I was at the racecourse for the first event of the year when I took the picture you can see. It was a lovely day with a large crowd all set to have a good time. Insights into the preparation were clear – the grass was well tended, the fences looking perfectly even, the white railings glistening in the early afternoon sun and the staff from the course all noticeable as they wore green blazers.

 It got me thinking about a whole range of things – how well managed the event was. The training by the owners and jockeys so their horses would perform well on the day. The leadership hoped for once the starting tape had risen. The celebration for those who won, the reviewing by those who didn't.

It also struck me that of the many that took part in each race, only the ones at the front of the race would be remembered – so all of their preparation would be recognised whereas the ones who finished down the field would only be forgotten by those who ripped up their losing race ticket and headed to the book makers for the next race, the next opportunity.

The difference is so often small – winning by a nose. So some questions:

- When did you last win a deal, a promotion a contract? And was it by a nose or a clear win?

- When did you last lose out to a competitor – and was that only by a nose? What more could you have done?

- Are you remaining 'fit' by undertaking on-going training and development?

If you are not investing in individual, team and business development – in leadership development, in management development, perhaps we need to speak.

Isn't it important to keep your nose out in front?

A path of least resistance…..

The other day I was walking along a footpath and saw the shortcut in the picture. This had been created by people walking from a nearby car park to the path. Whilst a little annoying that people had decided to make this unofficial path, because they were not prepared to walk the long way round, it got me thinking. The path did go in a loop and the new path was the shortest distance. And whilst the proper surfaced path only increased the distance walked by a small amount it was clearly sufficient to be enough to make a difference.

You may also see in the picture that the people who cut the grass had the insights to cut the area to the sides of the new path. This made the route clearer to walk on even though it was not the 'official' path.

I was interested to see that no signs had been erected directing people to the 'correct' route. Nor a small barrier or fence placed to discourage people – in fact quite the reverse.

How often have we been somewhere where there is every attempt to dissuade customers from doing things? You know the sort – 'no cheques accepted here', 'no mobile phones', 'do not walk on the grass', 'please keep to the foot path'.

This got me thinking about how we treat our customers or clients – are we telling them what we don't what them to do, signs screaming out at the behaviours **we** don't want. Rather than noticing what **they** want….and then responding to their wishes in a positive way.

It also reminded me of the time I was in a restaurant in France when my guest requested fresh fruit for dessert – the waitress was very brusque saying that there was none on the menu. The desserts on the menu were all complex creations but far too rich.

When the chef was eventually asked, a wonderful fresh fruit selection was prepared. We were being told what we could not have rather than considering a customer's request that could be met – and the teamwork to create a result was not high for the waitress. I would add that the request was in good French and polite.

- So have you anything that you try and make the customer do when they have indicated that they would prefer to do something differently?

- Are you clearing a path to allow a customer free passage to your products and services?

- Does their shortcut highlight something that you could do differently, or something additional you could offer?

Perhaps it is worth looking at your business with the eyes of a customer once in a while and see what routes you could shorten – what insights you could gain!

Perhaps each could be a shortcut to a better customer relationship rather than a sign warning them off.

Insights Discovery

After a weekend investing some time and money in my own development, Monday saw me at a further day of development in my role as mentor for Insights Discovery – which is probably the best behavioural profiling instrument that is available on the market today across the world. It is certainly one of the most accurate. I love the product as it can create such major learning and development at an individual, team and business level. And whilst easy to understand, it has massive depth.

I have used many other instruments in the past and nothing comes close for the impact I can create when helping in management and leadership development. One of the uses I make is with deep work at a one: one level. I often struggle with the terms coaching and executive coaching as they really have become so generic for all kinds of work. My work focuses on developing people to the highest level and more often than not a blended approach is used.

The day was great personal development for me too – there is always something new to learn. A different 'take' to something that we have been using. Something new to learn about myself too. It will seem excessive to some to take 4 days out of a busy business life. To lose a 3-day weekend tucked up in a conference centre and then have another day away from the business. Well if it improves your game it is well worth it.

We have all heard to story of the lumberjack who worked longer and longer hours to chop the same number of trees down – failing to realise time used to sharpen the axe would have kept performance at peak level. Similar to Coveys 'sharpen the saw' in the Seven Habits of Highly Effective People.

So:

- Are you keeping your axe sharp?

- Are you investing in your own development?

- Have you and your team got your insights discovery profile?

- Are you up to date?

If not, perhaps we need to speak.

Seasonal impressions do count…..

My last article got me thinking about the impression we make. I have written elsewhere about first impressions and indeed have a fantastic special report on the subject too in my product section at the back of this book (by the way 'fantastic' is the word of a client not mine!).

No, what I was interested in is the way the changing seasons create changes in the way we present ourselves. As we move from the colder weather to the warmer, and on some days hot conditions, all manner of changes are to be seen on our streets and in businesses in the area of dress code.

Some people see it as on opportunity to bring out their summer clothes. Others continue with their winter wear but just wear less. Whilst others just abandon any attempt to look tidy thinking that the advent of summer is an excuse for untidy dress and presentation.

How does this work in your business? Do you use it as a time to let standards slip? All that development in brand and image falling by the wayside?

Interesting questions for many organisations, and a subject area so seldom discussed on a management development programme, rarely on any leadership development programme – and yet.....huge amounts of money are spent on brand development. There seems to be little congruence for some businesses.

So perhaps a final question – do you consider the seasonal impact on your business image?

That could differentiate you from the crowd – positively and also negatively – now that is your choice.

Henley inspires teamwork.....

I was at a conference at Henley Business School, on the Thames, a couple of days ago and had a very useful day. The learning was top notch with good speakers and many thoughts that inspired new thinking. The variety of fellow attendees was as good as ever too, with some people flying in just for the day. I always think when that happens there is some serious commitment to their own continuing professional development.

During the day we had plenty of time to share thoughts with others who had attended but sadly not everyone, as there were about 80 people.

At the end of the day, after the sessions had ended, we went for a late afternoon boat trip on the river – well the world famous Henley Regatta was taking place – and far too good an opportunity to miss on such a wonderful summer day! The picture you see is of one of the races with what are called 'coxed eights', which got me thinking about an excerpt from a book I use when working with teams. It is as follows:

> "I used to say that an English team was a contradiction and a paradox, a paradox best illustrated by a rowing eight on the river. There are eight people going backwards as fast as they can without speaking to each other. Steering is in the hands of the one person who cannot row, because you put a chap in charge who cannot do the job….."

On hearing this, an Olympic oarsman commented:

> "How do you think we can go backwards so fast without talking to each other, unless we know each other terribly well, unless we have total confidence in each other's ability to do the job we are supposed to do, including that little chap who can't row, who is steering, unless we are all absolutely dedicated to getting to the end of the course before anybody else does, and winning the race.
>
> ….If you know each other very well and trust each other completely then you do not have to talk while you are doing the job. Everybody can get on with the job in hand. This gives you total commitment to the common goal."

From:- The search for meaning – Charles Handy

So:

- How well do you know each other in your team?

- How good is your trust?

- Do you play to strengths?

- In fact what are the strengths everyone has?

There are some great ways to enhance your leadership skills, your professional development, and gain a greater insight into team development. Is now a good time? I would be delighted to offer some thoughts.

Is your management development worth the price of a tea?

A while ago I wrote an article on the fact that most managers spend more on their daily coffee than they do on their own management development. I thought at the time that this would cause a few raised eyebrows. It did.

I also hoped that people would realise that it does not take that much money to make a difference in one's own development. Clearly I was wrong!

I have been doing some very casual research recently regarding how much people are prepared to spend. The general answer is very little. A rather more comprehensive review shows that the extremes are vast. I have met with people who are investing many £000s (these are the exceptions, by the way) and many who consider it a cost and spend nothing at all.

I have also discovered that it is the people who are employed who spend the least. They have a mind-set that it is their employer's responsibility to ensure that they are developed well enough for the role they perform. In 'transactional analysis' language this is called a child:parent relationship, with the employee not taking responsibility for their actions. The ideal relationship is adult:adult, by the way.

I had first-hand experience of this a few weeks ago when I was attending a business seminar with about 200 other people. One of the people I met praised one of my publications saying how useful it is and it had really helped in his new role. I was delighted with the feedback and asked him where he had got a copy from. Apparently his manager had passed the publication to him. A few minutes later we were joined by the more senior manager who had passed over his copy of the publication I had gifted to him a year or so before. I teased and remarked that in his new senior position couldn't he have afforded to buy a new copy for his more junior colleague.....it is only £5.

Apparently their budgets do not stretch to this sort of expenditure, something I was rather shocked about in view of the size of the business. I also teased that he could have purchased a copy himself and passed it over......

Well, I am writing this article in a Cotswold tea room. The cost of afternoon tea is £7.95, not an unreasonable price in this day and age, and in such a beautiful part of Britain. I am sure many people think little of indulging in this short-lived luxury.

Sadly it seems that few see the £5 as a worthwhile investment in their mind. Interesting!

As Benjamin Franklin said "An investment in knowledge always pays the best interest"

So a thought or four to ponder:

1. Is your afternoon tea more important that an investment in yourself?

2. If your employer is not providing for your development, who is?

3. If you are not developing yourself, at what point does your value in the market place start to diminish?

4. …..and at what stage do you start to be unemployable?

Some tough questions I am sure. You could have a peep at the growing range of publications all written to help in your own personal and management development – details at the end of this book or on the website.

Now anyone for tea?

Are you taking 'note'……?

I was having a saxophone lesson the other evening and learning to play a series of test pieces to develop my speed and skill at reading the notes and then playing what I saw.

My teacher, a very experienced player and teacher was ribbing me a little about my continued desire to make sure that I played every note right. The point he was making was that at my stage of playing it did not matter if I made mistakes. It is better to keep up the flow of the music and not to worry about missed notes – either forgotten or just wrongly played.

He illustrated this to me some weeks before where he played a piece where every note he played correctly, but the wrong length. He then played the piece with the correct pace and length notes, but every note was wrong. It was strange as the piece was unrecognisable when he played it first but recognisable on the second playing. Interesting!

After teasing me a little more, during my lesson he said if a note is wrong or missed don't worry, it has hit the floor and is gone – keep moving forward. You cannot go back and put the note back in you have to keep moving forward. All but the best players make mistakes and in many cases people don't notice – they do notice if you stop, as I had done!

Now where is this taking us?

Well, how often in our world of work do we make a mistake and then stop, trying to correct things, when so often it does not matter. So often we do stop, we try and go back and put things right….and so often for no purpose at all. Sometimes going back and trying to amend things makes the situation much worse.

- So how often have you made a mistake and you have frozen?

- How often have you made a mistake only to spend so much more time trying to rectify something that did not really matter?

- How often have you 'worried' the issue far more by attempting to cover your tracks? (When perhaps a simple 'sorry' would have allowed us to move forward rather than inflame the issue!)

Imperfect action is usually far better than no action.

Now will you take 'note' and let your music flow?

Be 'back wise'....

Some years ago I had a major back problem which caused me a lot of issues. I spent a lot of time and money investigating what I could do to avoid surgery and get back to full health. After much trial and often painful error I managed to establish what worked.

I was at a business event a couple of years ago with over 100 other people and mentioned what had happened and that I was fine now. I was very surprised by the reaction - clearly many people in the room knew people they cared about who had back problems too. Well, to cut to the chase, the enthusiasm in the room was so high that I was asked to write what I had done down in a book. At last I have now done this.

Firstly, whilst it has taken many long hours to write the book, I have really enjoyed the process. I am also surprised just how much I have written based on what I did and what I now do to keep my back in good shape. It is all straight forward, written in non-medical language and shares what I did to regain my health.

So what is the business importance of this? Quite simple – back ache and back related issues are a major source of ill health absenteeism. And in my view, much of this absenteeism could be avoided if we all took a 'back wise' approach to the way we live.

If you run your own business you cannot afford to be ill and if you have any employees, you want them fit too. If you manage or lead a business of a larger size, absenteeism can be very costly too. And that does not allow for the personal suffering anyone with back pain goes through.

Perhaps my new book is worth a peep so have a look at the website: **www.thebackchampion.com** The content is weighty, the price certainly isn't!

So be 'back wise'.

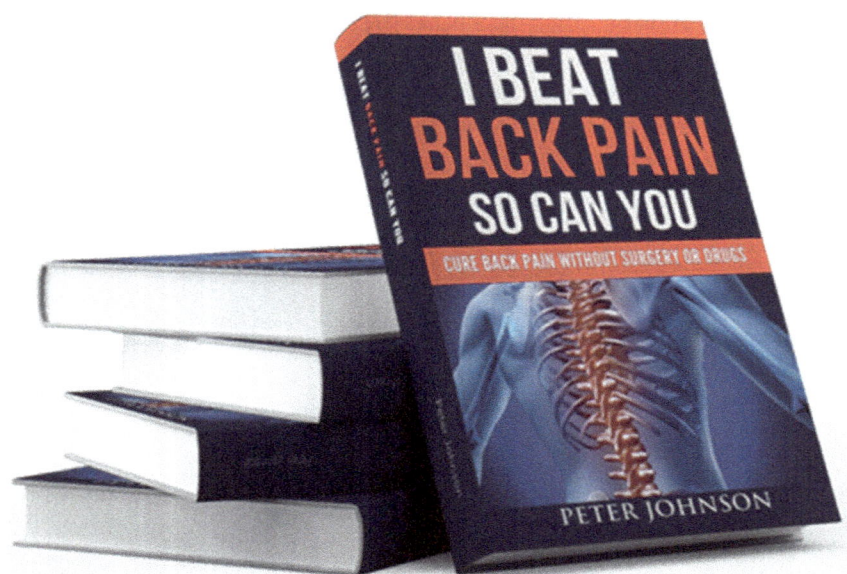

Learning and development is key....

I have recently been finalising some new learning of my own. I usually manage to undertake one main programme a year with a series of other shorter events that I attend. Some are good, some less so – always there is some new learning and development for my portfolio. As I grow older my thirst for learning increases, keeping my own skills sharp and up to date are important for the work I do and the clients I work with. I also have a lot of fun with it too.

Sometimes when we are in the midst of things, we can wonder why we started though.....as I found out a few weeks ago. I had committed to complete a major piece of learning this year.

So a couple of months ago, I was completing what is call an 'open book' examination paper (so called as you can use the books you have been studying). It was a paper we could complete at home too so all seems a little odd compared with my early education when two or three years of learning all hinged on a three hour examination.

This paper took me over 30 hours to complete – which apparently is normal. It would have been so easy to just give up, head off with some friends or watched the TV. One of the things that did inspire me was the diversity of our student group – young and not so young and from many diverse work backgrounds all sharing in a common interest. There seemed few barriers between us as we worked to our goal with a vast amount of peer support and encouragement. Just fantastic.

It is interesting that when we are working towards something and sharing a common interest and goal all other issues seem to be secondary. Something that I had known all along, but had unfortunately forgotten. This was a brilliant reminder and rather humbling too.

So perhaps it's a good time to think about what you may have forgotten that could be valuable. Could it be that there are some great people you are ignoring who are also working towards a common goal? Pick up the phone or drop them an email, they may just value your help in their own learning and development too.

Positive realism –a useful tonic……?

I was sitting in a café in Exeter, England with a friend after a business meeting I had just completed. We were discussing the state of the economy and the world of work generally. It is quite clear that there are many problems in businesses at the moment with uncertainty caused by the general economic fragility of the western world. It is sad to note the impact this has on people and the dampening of enthusiasm when we live in a world that has advanced so far. Significant blame is laid at the door or our national leaders, and those who lead our organisations, about their inability to act or do what is considered by others as the 'right' thing.

The person I was speaking with is normally upbeat, and this was no exception. In a world where our news seems to survive on gloom and troubled stories, it is always refreshing to share time with someone who has a positive view of life. This is no false 'think positive' attitude that ignores the realities of life – more of an approach that focuses on looking at the up-side of any situation until it is clear that action is needed to correct a poor course of action. It is also quite refreshing as so many seem to complain when things could be much worse.

I have found that people who are constantly taking the negative view of things either end up lonely or mix with people who also take a pessimistic view of life. Spending time with negative people can be so draining.

- So in your business are you taking a positive approach even though things could be better or are you declaring daily gloom?

- What impact do you think this has on any potential client or customer?

- What impact do you think this may be having on the people who are near and dear to you in business and in our wider life?

You will know the answer –and if it is the answer you would like. If a little more spring is needed in your step can I suggest you make the effort to do so? You will feel better and so will those around you......and one of those may well be an important new customer.

The cycle of learning....

I was in Oxford. England a couple of days ago, meeting up with a client I had not seen for a while. As ever, the conversation was good and it is always interesting to hear what they are doing with their management development work and the training of their large workforce. It is also interesting to see what leadership development they are undertaking too. These are areas of my expertise, interest, and what I do.

I find it interesting that so many people at the top of businesses are very cautious of their own development whilst prepared to invest in people lower down the ladder. One of the things I have noticed over my many years in business is the reluctance of this 'learning culture' at the top of businesses. Now does this create an atmosphere of learning within an organisation or is it seen as something the leaders 'do' to their people?

Oxford is known the world over for its University (in fact many colleges that make up the overall University) and its excellence as a place of learning. The enthusiasm for learning is visible during the academic semesters and even outside these times there is interest and pride in the various colleges. The memorabilia that people are keen to purchase. The peeping behind the closed doors and into the inner 'quads' that hide behind old large wooden doors. The photographs that are captured by people from around the world to share on their return home. The rows of bicycles that meet you at each turn, that in college time are many more, as students of all ages journey around the city for their lectures.

Now questions that made me think:

- Are you a spectator of learning and development, just recycling your past learning?

- Is it something you 'peddle' to your people?

- When was the last time you got on your own mental exercise bicycle to help in your own development?

If these questions made you feel uncomfortable, perhaps it would be a good time to speak. If you are used to being in the learning saddle well done.....you are in the minority.

Final Comment

Throughout this book you have been gently challenged to take action and review aspects of your world of work and non-work.

My hope is that you take action, even if only on one point. By so doing you will have moved forward and are now further on your journey - automatically creating new horizons.

New horizons to give new perspective, new vitality, new focus.

Enjoy the journey.......

Acknowledgements

No book surfaces without the nudge, support and enthusiasm of others. There is always a moment of doubt that could stifle any further action. The resulting work-in-progress ending up slumbering in the depths of a hard drive of a long forgotten computer. In dusty notepads, or in photographs that never see the light of day.

So a huge thank you for the people who have provide support in giving this book life. There are far too many people who have provided thought and material to mention – people who may have accidently slowed me down as I sped through my daily tasks. That chance slowing enabling me to see something I had missed. The question of "have you seen….?", and so much more.

One person stands out whom I would like to thank, albeit she sadly is now only with us in spirit, and that is a dear friend Dame Margaret Anstee. She introduced me to the wonders of South America where we enjoyed numerous evenings talking into the early hours whilst warming ourselves front of wonderful a log fire, at her home, on the shores of Lake Titicaca, in Bolivia. Magical.

I would like to thank Stephanie Hale the founder of the Oxford Literacy Consultancy for the wisdom shared and encouraging matter of fact way that she makes things feel so much more achievable. Becky Gladwin for the support in pulling things together, and a small army of other people without whose input this book would not have seen the light of day.

I would also like to thank Louis Parsons for the artwork that creates the covers of this series. Each form part of a series called The Soul Notes. He is the master pioneer of a new form of art he calls SoulScapes which celebrate, and reach into the essence of who we are.

I would especially like to thank my parents. For a father who was a great photographer and taught me to look beyond the camera lens at what I was going record – I know I have abused that wisdom in a number of pictures in this book. For a mother and the way she always makes the simple so valued, for slowing life and treasuring the moment when everything else rushes past in a blur.

A large thank you for the many instances where I have noticed something because someone said something, did something, moved something that caused me to take note. Many of the pieces in this book are because of someone doing something that enabled me to create a patchwork of observations and thoughts.

And my appreciation for those who have reached this far in the book; you keep the precious gift of reading alive in a world where so many who can read, fail to read even one book a year. A travesty when so many, still, have yet to have to opportunity to read.

Other Publications

For more publications by Peter Johnson head over to:

www.PeterJohnsonOnline.com

This book forms part of a growing series of publications, which focus on business, health and wellbeing.

Business Coaching & Consulting

Peter Johnson works with individuals, teams and business to make positive lasting change utilising coaching, mentoring facilitation, speaking and consulting. He has worked with many large 'brand names' he has also work with many much smaller organisations, including charities.

His workshops and programmes are bespoke and are designed for immediate impact.

He loves working with business and people who have reached a plateau and need that bit of extra oomph from someone who can become a trusted advisor and confidant.

For more help and to seek advice, go to:

www.PeterJohnsonOnline.com

Peter Johnson Bio

Peter has a firm belief that everyone has unfathomed potential, often quoting: "The greatest waste in the world is the difference between what we are and what we could become".

He chose to leave a successful high-level corporate career to deliver lasting benefit through executive coaching, mentoring, facilitation, speaking and consulting. He also teaches a programme for other consultants, trainers, coaches and people looking to develop a freelance consultancy career. He has held many Chair and Trustee charity roles too.

He is highly qualified, an alumnus of two top international business schools and the world's 1st person accredited in a specialist area of personality psychology. Peter continues to invest heavily in his ongoing education.

The Institute of Directors recognised his expertise by awarding Director of the Year finalist twice; he is also an award-winning author.

To contact Peter to see if he can help you, your team, or your business achieve excellence do send him an email at:

peter@peterjohnsononline.com

Notes

Lightning Source UK Ltd.
Milton Keynes UK
UKHW02f0229280218
318616UK00006B/51/P